52 SHORT REFLECTIONS FROM
SEARCHING FOR THE GOD OF GRACE

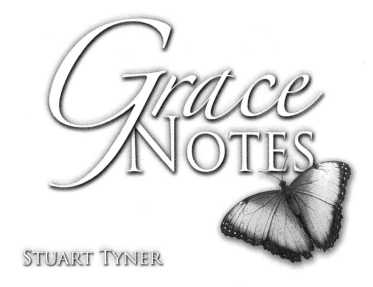

Grace NOTES

STUART TYNER

Pacific Press® Publishing Association
Nampa, Idaho
Oshawa, Ontario, Canada
www.pacificpress.com

Designed by Steve Lanto
Cover photo by dreamstime.com

Copyright © 2006 by
Pacific Press® Publishing Association
All rights reserved
Printed in the United States of America

ISBN 13: 978-0-8163-2204-6
ISBN 10: 0-8163-2204-X

06 07 08 09 10 · 5 4 3 2 1

A Word to the Reader

We Christians seem to find it so difficult to resist the idea that we can somehow blend taking responsibility for our own salvation with Jesus' gift of atonement. Part of it is the very human desire to be independent—"I can do it myself." Part of it is fear—fear that putting everything in the hands of grace will cause us to become careless about being obedient followers of Jesus. And part of it is because, in our heart of hearts, we feel that we don't really deserve Jesus' love or His salvation or His grace. And, of course, we don't. If we deserved it, it wouldn't be grace, would it?

The fact of the matter is that when it comes to salvation and acceptance with God, His grace stands above and before and in place of anything else. Pastor Stuart Tyner opens his book, *Searching for the God of Grace,* with an original poem—"Before the Beginning." The first verse of that poem expresses the primacy of grace like this:

Before our birth, both yours and mine, there was an invitation;
Before we ever sought His face or tried to earn His favor;
Before we knew to worship Him, or righteousness to savor;
Before our praise, before our works, before our pulse, was grace.

Easy to say, but so hard to live! The glorious treasure of God's grace, inexhaustible, valuable beyond measure, is far too often ignored, refused, locked up, and buried. In his book, Tyner tries to uncover the treasure—the spectacular riches of God's grace. The book you are holding contains 52 brief reflections on grace—each made up of a quotation taken from the book *Searching for the God of Grace* paired with a short statement from Ellen White. But although they may not take long to read, these reflections will provide food for thought for days. Think of the 52 readings on grace in this little book as weekly "booster shots" to help you maintain your immunity against the subtle spiritual disease of self-sufficiency.

And if you are intrigued by these quotations and would like to read *Searching for the God of Grace* in its entirety—look for information on the last page of this book.

The Publisher

1

*G*race is our choicest treasure. . . . It is the revealing of the honor of God, an unfolding of His glory. —ELLEN WHITE, *IN HEAVENLY PLACES*, 220.

This is the record of how God chose us in Christ "before the creation of the world" (Ephesians 1:4), how we have been adopted to be children of the King to the praise of God's glorious grace, "which he has freely given us in the One he loves" in accordance with the riches of His grace (Ephesians 1:6, 7). . . . It's about how our names have been written "in the book of life belonging to the Lamb" (Revelation 13:8). It's about how this treasure and this treasure alone can reorient our identity in our deepest reality.—p. 19.

2

*S*o surely as there never was a time when God was not, so surely there never was a moment when it was not the delight of the eternal mind to manifest His grace to humanity.—Ellen White, *Signs of the Times,*

June 12, 1901.

The treasure is already ours, but it's never forced upon us. We can refuse it, ignore it, trample on it, attempt to obscure it, or lock it up and bury it. We can be afraid of grace, as so many have been throughout history and as so many continue to be. . . . However, in spite of all our efforts to bury it, the treasure remains.—p. 21.

3

*G*od rejoices to bestow His grace upon us, not because we are worthy, but because we are so utterly unworthy. Our only claim to His mercy is our great need.—ELLEN WHITE, *THE MINISTRY OF HEALING*, 161.

$\mathcal{T}$he impulse to try to change God's mind is as ancient as Cain, as persistent as Sarah's laughter, as quick as Moses' grasping credit for bringing water from a rock. Our words betray us. "Make me like one of Your hired servants," we insist, speaking the language of merit so stubbornly that we miss the warmth of our Father's welcoming embrace. . . . It's almost as if we were running away from the gospel, as if we were afraid of grace, not wanting to be *that* rich, *that* forgiven, *that* assured.—p. 41.

4

*I*t is not possible to effect anything in our standing before God or in the gift of God to us through
creature merit. . . . Salvation, then, . . . must be
wholly of grace.—ELLEN WHITE, *FAITH AND WORKS*, 19.

*I*n the culture of achievement in which we live, my natural reflexes and trained sensibilities persistently resist the good news of grace. . . . Frequently, . . . I approach God with my hands full of something of my own to use in the bargaining. . . . I am so capable of interposing myself into the transaction: my commitment, my obedience, my high standards.—p. 41

5

The sacrifice of Christ as an atonement for sin is the great truth around which all other truths cluster.—ELLEN WHITE, *GOSPEL WORKERS*, 315.

*I*n our sincere efforts to respond to God's call to be peculiar, distinctive people, we must not rush past the core definition of our existence or push it into the periphery of our experience. . . . Whenever we stray from our foundation in the everlasting gospel and make any other ground our central position, we come perilously close to missing completely the point of *the truth as it is in Jesus.*

—p. 42.

6

*T*o be a child of God means to be constantly receiving grace.—ELLEN WHITE, *REVIEW AND HERALD*, JANUARY 8, 1895.

$\mathcal{G}$race is not the beginning point of the Christian journey; it is the road upon which journeying Christians walk day by day, moment by moment. Grace is not a robe Christians put on in order to be correctly dressed; it is the air Christians breathe in order to live.—p. 45.

7

The Lord saw our fallen condition; He saw our need of grace, and because He loved our souls, He has given us grace and peace. Grace means favor to one who is undeserving, to one who is lost.

—Ellen White, *Selected Messages*, book 1, 347.

*G*od is full of grace. He hates the sinful things sinners do, but He doesn't hate *sinners*. He hates their evil influence. He hates the hurt they cause. He hates seeing children suffer. But he loves the people who do those terrible things. They are His children too. He longs to change their hearts. His grace extends to all sinners, to all of us.—p. 61.

8

*W*e owe everything to God's free grace. Grace in the covenant ordained our adoption. Grace in the Saviour effected our redemption, our regeneration, and our exaltation to heirship with Christ.

—Ellen White, *In Heavenly Places*, 34.

*T*he invitation not to be afraid of grace is as clear in the Old Testament as it is in the New Testament. "This is what the Lord says—he who created you, . . . who formed you, O Israel: 'Fear not, for I have redeemed you; I have summoned you by name; you are mine' " (Isaiah 43:1). . . . "God has chosen you as a cherished personal treasure," Moses underlines the point, "not because you were more numerous than other peoples" or "because of your righteousness or your integrity," but "because He loved you" (see Deuteronomy 7:6; 9:5; 7:8). . . . No wonder Peter can say that the Old Testament prophets "spoke of the grace that was to come" (1 Peter 1:10).—pp. 66, 67.

9

*T*he closer you come to Jesus, the more faulty
you will appear in your own eyes; for your vision
will be clearer, and your imperfections will be seen
in broad and distinct contrast to His perfect

nature.—Ellen White, *Steps to Christ*, 64.

Gideon's story is able to make us wise unto salvation. It's not a story about what God can do with three hundred soldiers. It's about the total impossibility of the situation. . . . Gideon's story is not about a brilliant military strategy or a courageous, dedicated fighting force; it's about grace—about God doing for humans that which is impossible for us to do for ourselves. God saves us the same way He delivers Israel from the Midianites—without the help of our numerical superiority. "Stand still and see the salvation of the Lord."—p. 68.

10

$\mathcal{J}$esus imparts all the powers, all the grace, all the penitence, all the inclination, all the pardon of sins, in presenting His righteousness for man to grasp by living faith.—ELLEN WHITE, *FAITH AND WORKS*, 24.

The story of David and Goliath is able to make us wise unto salvation. The salvation lesson looms larger than Goliath's shadow: In a moment, Christ, our Champion, wades into earth's dry riverbed, defeats the enemy, and then turns to all of us standing on the sidelines and gives us the victory. In this Old Testament story, God once again tries to teach us the definition of grace: God doing for humans that which is impossible for us to do for ourselves. God saves us the same way. He defeats the Goliaths and then gives us the victory. "Stand still and see the salvation of the Lord."—p. 69.

11

It is the gospel of the grace of God alone that can uplift the soul. The contemplation of the love of God manifested in His Son will stir the heart and arouse the powers of the soul as nothing else can.

—Ellen White, *The Desire of Ages*, 478.

*T*he gospel of grace is all about resting in the saving presence of Jesus in the cosmic battles of the great controversy. Of course, God is there throughout our earthly journey—in the wakening desire to accept His love, in the daily struggles of our everyday existence, in our growing realization that we don't have to be afraid of grace. But in that first dawning understanding that we are a blessed, chosen people (Deuteronomy 7:6; 14:2), we realize that it is so because God has freely given us His glorious grace and guaranteed our salvation (2 Samuel 23:5).—pp. 77, 78.

12

*T*he soul that responds to the grace of God shall be like a watered garden. His health shall spring forth speedily; his light shall rise in obscurity, and the glory of the Lord shall be seen upon him.

—ELLEN WHITE, *THE MINISTRY OF HEALING*, 100.

*B*iblical rest envelops us, makes us feel secure (Psalm 16:9), and gives us a sustaining realization of God's unfailing love (Psalm 33:22). "My soul finds rest in God alone," David reflects, "my salvation comes from him" (Psalm 62:1). "My people will live in peaceful dwelling places," Isaiah reassures us with the words of God, "in secure homes, in undisturbed places of rest" (Isaiah 32:18). We rest because "[our] Redeemer is strong" (Jeremiah 50:34). Every Sabbath should be like that. Every time we move forward with God at the center of our lives, that's what it's supposed to be like.—p. 78.

13

God's grace and the law of his kingdom are in
perfect harmony; they walk hand in hand.

—Ellen White, *Review and Herald*, September 15, 1896.

*T*he gospel of grace asks us to distinguish between two views of the Christian life. One view understands Christian behavior as a heartfelt response to the wholly unmerited gift of salvation. The other view of the Christian life suggests that what we do contributes to the process of salvation—a process that hopefully, if we work hard enough and make enough right decisions, will result in God rewarding us for our good work. . . . Grace is a moment-by-moment reminder that God's role in our salvation is to save us, and our role is to quit trying to save ourselves.—p. 79.

14

*H*e who is trying to become holy by his own works in keeping the law, is attempting an impossibility. . . . It is the grace of Christ alone, through faith that can make us holy.—ELLEN WHITE,

STEPS TO CHRIST, 60.

*W*hat we are to cease doing on the Sabbath has always been so much bigger than not washing dishes or not riding bicycles. . . . The Sabbath is about ceasing our attempts to be God! . . . . Ceasing work on the Sabbath is about declaring our acceptance of grace, about celebrating that God has given us the gift of eternal life, about resting in the assurance of salvation, about distinguishing between God's work of giving grace and our work of receiving grace.—p. 81.

15

The idea of doing anything to merit the grace of pardon is fallacy from beginning to end.

—ELLEN WHITE, *FAITH AND WORKS*, 24.

36

*H*ow in the world did Sabbathkeepers manage to turn the Sabbath into the badge of righteousness by works? How did God's chosen people transform the tabernacle into a fearful symbol of judgment? How did the already redeemed redefine the gospel of grace and make salvation something we could earn?—p. 82.

16

*A*bundant grace has been provided that the believing soul may be kept free from sin; for all heaven, with its limitless resources, has been placed at our command.—Ellen White, *Selected Messages*, book 1, 394.

*S*alvation is one of the Bible's larger-than-life words. It connotes full deliverance from all the ravages of sin we experience in this enemy-held territory we call planet Earth—all the pain and sorrow and destruction, all the atrocity, the guilt, the hopelessness (Revelation 21:4) . . . all the discouragement that almost overwhelms us in this world. Salvation delivers us from all of that. *Jesus* delivers us from all of that. When you hear the word *salvation,* think big—think Second Coming clouds and thunder and lightning, think heaven, think eternity.—p. 91.

17

In the love of God has been opened the most marvelous vein of precious truth, and the treasures of the grace of Christ are laid open before the church and the world. . . . What a loss it is to the soul who understands the strong claims of the law, and who yet fails to understand the grace of Christ which doth much more abound!

—ELLEN WHITE, *SELECTED MESSAGES*, BOOK 1, 384.

We frequently talk about salvation as if its chief purpose is to deliver us from *immediate* temptation. As if John the Baptist has said to us, "Behold the Lamb of God who takes away the desire to eat too much *Special K* loaf." . . . Assuredly, deliverance from immediate temptation is also a work of God's grace in our lives. But the salvation we are speaking of . . . , *biblical* salvation, is big-picture salvation, capital "S" Salvation, the act of God, and God alone that by His grace give us an *eternal* home in heaven.—p. 91.

*G*od's supply of grace is waiting the demand of every sinsick soul. It will heal every spiritual disease. . . . It is the gospel remedy for everyone who believes.—ELLEN WHITE, *IN HEAVENLY PLACES*, 34.

*G*race is the good Samaritan who knows no national boundary or cultural bias, but who rescues and heals because our need is so immediate and real. Grace is the bandage that binds the wounds when we can't stop the bleeding. Grace is the oil and wine that heal the hurts when we can't even dull the pain. Grace is the donkey that carries us to the place where we can heal, the place we can't reach by ourselves. Grace is the money that pays the expenses for us when we don't have even a pocketful of change (Luke 10:30-35).—p. 93.

19

*T*he riches of the grace of Christ are without limit. They are sufficient to fill every heart with wisdom and sanctified judgment, creating an atmosphere of grace, real and enjoyable.

—ELLEN WHITE, *PACIFIC UNION RECORDER,* AUGUST 1, 1901.

*A*ll of us are justified exactly the same way, "freely by his grace through the redemption that came by Christ Jesus" (Romans 3:24). We are justified "by faith apart from observing the law" (verse 28; Galatians 3:24). We are justified by Christ's blood (Romans 5:9). We are justified in the name of the Lord Jesus Christ (1 Corinthians 6:11). We are justified by His grace (Titus 3:7).

—p. 108.

*N*othing but the righteousness of Christ can entitle us to one of the blessings of the covenant of grace. . . . We must not think that our own merits will save us; Christ is our only hope of salvation.

—ELLEN WHITE, *PATRIARCHS AND PROPHETS,* 431.

*J*ohn the revelator spoke to the people in the church of Philadelphia about Jesus as the One who " 'holds the key of David' " (Revelation 3:7). . . . Jesus holds the key that unlocks the palace of heaven. You and I don't have the key. We can't get in. Only Jesus can open the door. Jesus is the final authority as to who gets in. We don't make that decision. Only He does. And what He opens, no one can shut. Salvation is by grace alone because Jesus alone holds the key.—p. 123.

21

*P*recious Saviour! His grace is sufficient for the weakest; and the strongest must also have His grace or perish.—Ellen White,

Testimonies for the Church, vol. 1, 158.

It is often the case that those who find the least comfort in grace, those who argue against it most vehemently, those who most fear grace, are those who place the lowest estimate on the power of sin in their own lives. The sins of others are much more disagreeable than our own, we somehow reason—missing the reality that the doctrine of grace *begins* with a realization of our universal need for God's grace and our absolute inability to provide salvation for ourselves.

—p. 129.

*O*nly the covering which Christ Himself has provided can make us meet to appear in God's presence. This covering, the robe of His own righteousness, ... woven in the loom of heaven, has in it not one thread of human devising.

—ELLEN WHITE, *CHRIST'S OBJECT LESSONS,* 311.

Therefore, as God's chosen people, holy and dearly loved, clothe yourselves with compassion, kindness, humility, gentleness and patience" . . . ([Colossians 1:]12-14, emphasis supplied).

The "holy and dearly loved" wear clothes of compassion. Kindness, humility, gentleness, and patience look natural on the people who realize God has chosen them. Try to wear the clothes on your own, before you accept God's grace, and they

 become "filthy rags" (Isaiah 64:6).—p. 135.

23

*D*ivine grace is the great element of saving power; without it all human effort is unavailing.

—ELLEN WHITE, *THE FAITH I LIVE BY*, 94.

*A*ny and every attempt to secure salvation without grace . . . minimizes the condition for standing in the presence of a perfect, holy God (1 Samuel 6:20; Psalm 24:3, 4). It contradicts the Bible's insistence that *all of us* have sinned (Romans 3:23). It denies the Bible's conclusion that *all of us* need a Savior (Romans 3:24; 5:6-10). It fails the gospel requirement that what God does for us must be good news (Luke 2:10; Acts 5:42). Salvation by willpower doesn't work. Never has. Never will.

—p. 144.

24

You cannot hallow His name, you cannot represent Him to the world, unless in life and character you represent the very life and character of God. This you can do only through the acceptance of the grace and righteousness of Christ.—Ellen White,

God's Amazing Grace, 94.

$\mathcal{T}$he major difference [between justification and sanctification] is that justification is about salvation and sanctification is not about salvation. Justification is about God's grace forgiving us and accepting us and making us a member of His family. Sanctification is about growing up in the family, learning how to live a life of praise, and overcoming the temptations that so easily entice us to the pigsties.—p. 153.

*O*ur churches are dying for the want of teaching on the subject of righteousness by faith in Christ.

—ELLEN WHITE, *GOSPEL WORKERS*, 301.

*I*magine if you entered every day not knowing if your salvation was sure. Imagine driving to work or school hoping that you've confessed all your sins and really were forgiven, just in case you have an accident and your life ends. . . .

Imagine having to ignore one Scripture passage after another—passages like Romans 5:8: "God demonstrates his own love for us in this: While we were still *sinners,* Christ died for us" (emphasis supplied here and in the following texts). . . . And Ephesians 2:4, 5: "God who is rich in mercy, made us alive with Christ *even when we were dead in transgressions*—it is by grace you have been saved."—p. 154.

Christ's favorite theme was the paternal tenderness and abundant grace of God.—ELLEN WHITE,

CHRIST'S OBJECT LESSONS, 40.

Salvation *is not about* avoiding hell but about living forever in the presence of Jesus, our Redeemer. The good news *is not about* what we do to avoid the wages of sin, but about what Jesus did to demonstrate God's endless love so that " 'whoever believes in him, shall not perish but have eternal life' " (John 3:16).—p. 155.

27

*T*he reward is not of works, lest any man should boast; but it is all of grace. . . . No one is privileged above another, nor can anyone claim the reward as a right.—ELLEN WHITE, *CHRIST'S OBJECT LESSONS,* 401, 402.

*W*hat we do in response to the grace God has freely given us is entirely another story, and a very important one. There is plenty of counsel in the Bible about praying and keeping the Sabbath and paying our tithe and about how to treat people we love and how to treat our enemies—*but it's not the story of how we receive salvation!*—p. 155.

28

*T*here is one great central truth to be kept ever before the mind in the searching of the Scriptures—Christ and Him crucified.—ELLEN WHITE,

THE FAITH I LIVE BY, 50.

$\mathcal{T}$he good news of the everlasting gospel is that salvation is not about what you and I do or don't do. It's not about what we eat or drink, what we wear or don't wear, how we treat the people we love or how we treat our enemies. Those concerns are the *result* of the gospel. The gospel is about God's grace.—p. 156.

*W*e can do nothing of ourselves. In all our helpless unworthiness we must trust in the merits of the crucified and risen Saviour.—ELLEN WHITE,

PATRIARCHS AND PROPHETS, 203.

A biblical understanding of salvation by grace alone through faith alone in Jesus Christ alone brings with it "the assurance of the believer's acceptance. It brings the joy of being reunited with God *now.* No matter how sinful one's past life, God pardons all sins, and we are no longer under the condemnation and curse of the law. Redemption has become a reality."*. . . We have the assurance of salvation now and in the judgment.—p. 183.

Seventh-day Adventists Believe . . . , (Silver Spring, Md.: General Conference Ministerial Association, 2005), p. 138.

30

Of all professing Christians, Seventh-day Adventists should be foremost in uplifting Christ before the world. . . . It is at the cross of Christ that mercy and truth meet together, and righteousness and peace kiss each other.

—ELLEN WHITE, *GOSPEL WORKERS,* 156.

*M*ost Adventist young people, as well as their older brothers and sisters, their parents and grandparents, continue to worry that grace will undermine our commitment to God's law, continue to be reluctant to express a full assurance of salvation. . . . It is high time for us to agree to reclaim our Reformation roots in our lives as well as on paper.—p. 183.

31

The church is the repository of the riches of the grace of Christ. . . . It is the theater of His grace, in which He delights to reveal His power to transform hearts.—ELLEN WHITE, *SONS AND DAUGHTERS OF GOD*, 13.

*A*ll the tasks of ministry in the community of faith would be more acceptable, more achievable, if we would remember that our place in the kingdom, our gifts for ministry, and our opportunities to minister are not self-generated. They are not a reward for our goodness. They are not a payment in return for our merits. Rather, they are another unmistakable evidence of the undying love, the stubborn grace, the unquenchable, favorable

disposition of a steadfast, tender, and compassionate God.—p. 201.

32

*N*othing but the grace of God can convict and convert the heart.—ELLEN WHITE, *COUNSELS ON HEALTH*, 23.

The issues of 1888 continue to be with us. Even the question of whether the church received or rejected the message remains a matter of debate. Nevertheless, the message of Christ's righteousness, the everlasting gospel of God's saving grace, was placed so firmly in a central position that no one can ever again discuss Adventist theology without referring to this cardinal, fundamental feature of our faith.—p. 209.

*O*nly through the blood of the Crucified One is there cleansing from sin. His grace alone can enable us to resist and subdue the tendencies of our fallen nature.—ELLEN WHITE, *THE MINISTRY OF HEALING*, 428.

*C*hrist is the end of the law (whatever law! any law!) for righteousness (Romans 10:4). Once we see Jesus face to face, we easily give up all the law-keeping we do to try to merit heaven, all law-keeping for justification, all law-keeping to make God love us more. " 'If righteousness could be gained through the law, Christ died for nothing!' " (Galatians 2:21). How could it possibly be clearer than that?—p. 210.

34

*T*he heart renewed by the Holy Spirit will bring forth "the fruits of the Spirit." Through the grace of Christ we shall live in obedience to the law of God written upon our hearts. Having the Spirit of Christ, we shall walk even as He walked.

—ELLEN WHITE, *PATRIARCHS AND PROPHETS*, 372.

*N*o wonder we Adventists don't need to be afraid of grace. We understand that the law has led us to Jesus (Galatians 3:24), where we are justified, saved, redeemed, ransomed, and brought back to life. And not by anything we have done, not even by our obedience to God's perfect law, but by grace alone, through faith alone, in Jesus Christ alone.—p. 210.

*T*he grace of God must sweep through the chambers of the mind, the imagination must have heavenly themes for contemplation, and every element of the nature must be purified and vitalized by the Spirit of God.—ELLEN WHITE, *GOD'S AMAZING GRACE*, 206.

*E*llen White not only talks about the grace that saves and justifies, but she also talks about the grace that transforms and sanctifies. *Justifying grace* is God's act of forgiving sinners and declaring that they will be treated just as if they never had sinned. *Sanctifying grace* is God's power working in our lives to change and mold us into His image.—p. 221.

36

What is more worthy to engross the mind than the plan of redemption? It is a subject that is exhaustless. The love of Jesus, the salvation offered to fallen man through His infinite love, holiness of heart, the precious, saving truth for these last days, the grace of Christ—these are subjects which may animate the soul.—ELLEN WHITE,

THE VOICE IN SPEECH AND SONG, 116.

*S*ome people will be unhappy with the suggestion that Ellen White's understanding grew, that she knew grace better as the days went by, that anyone called and used by God might mature in their comprehension or expression. But according to the way we Adventists view the doctrine of inspiration . . . God doesn't call someone to labor for Him—not even the writers of the Bible—and then reveal to them the totality of His character and will all at once, leaving nothing for them to learn.—p. 222.

37

*C*hrist has given to the church a sacred charge.
Every member should be a channel through which
God can communicate to the world the treasures
of His grace, the unsearchable riches of Christ.

—ELLEN WHITE, *THE ACTS OF THE APOSTLES,* 600.

*C*an we establish a grace orientation in our lives, our homes, our classrooms and churches, and still share the insights that build Christian character? Can these two fundamental emphases of Christianity—a central appreciation for everything God has done for us in Jesus and a consistent call to become more and more Christlike—coexist successfully? Or does one emphasis necessarily undermine the other?—p. 230.

38

*A*s your soul yearns after God, you will find more and still more of the unsearchable riches of His grace.—ELLEN WHITE, *ACTS OF THE APOSTLES,* 567.

*H*owever you say it, the reality is clear: It is God's saving grace *and nothing else* that gives us a new name and a new status. And that's what transforms our behavior! It is grace that makes us desire grace. It is grace that makes us want to grow in Jesus (2 Peter 3:18). It is the fact that we have been justified by grace alone that makes us interested in being sanctified.—p. 232.

39

*H*e cannot receive the riches of the grace of Christ without desiring to impart them to others.—Ellen White, *Review and Herald*, August 26, 1890.

*D*o we really want to become more and more like Jesus? If that is true, we can approach success in our efforts in *only one way:* We must grow *in grace.* It is only when grace is in the driver's seat, when grace is central, that we obey and overcome in the way we want to obey and overcome. And only then does character building produce the results we want.—p. 233.

*W*hen sin struggles for the mastery in your soul, and burdens the conscience, look to the Saviour. His grace is sufficient to subdue sin. Let your grateful heart, trembling with uncertainty, turn to Him.—ELLEN WHITE, *THE MINISTRY OF HEALING,* 85.

The more we talk about Jesus, the more we sing about His amazing grace, the more we model our ministry after His, the more we will be attracted to Jesus. The more we learn about Jesus the more we will appreciate the gospel of God's grace (Acts 20:24)—the good news of God's full acceptance of us in Jesus (Acts 15:8-11), His continuing faithfulness (Psalm 100:3-5), and His loving kindness (Titus 3:3-7). And the more we are attracted to the beauty of the character of Jesus, the more we will desire to be changed into His likeness.—p. 234.

41

The gospel of Christ is from beginning to end the gospel of saving grace. . . . Full and everlasting salvation is within the reach of every soul. Christ is waiting and longing to speak pardon, and impart the freely offered grace.—ELLEN WHITE, *EVANGELISM,* 552.

*G*race is the "great truth around which all other truths cluster. In order to be rightly understood and appreciated, every truth in the Word of God"—including the truth about how important it is for our characters to glorify our Father in heaven (Matthew 5:16)—"must be studied in the light that streams from the cross of Calvary."* It is grace that gives meaning and purpose to character building, not character building that illuminates grace. Come to Jesus first.—pp. 234, 235.

---

*Ellen White, *Gospel Workers,* p. 315.

*I*t is a good thing that the heart be established with grace. This is the ground of our steadfastness.—ELLEN WHITE,

TESTIMONIES FOR THE CHURCH, VOL. 1, 438.

*W*e grow in Jesus because we are His children, never in order to become His children (1 John 3:1). We behave with propriety so that people will glorify God (Matthew 5:16), not so that we can convince God to like us. We need to develop our characters so that we can honor God, not so that we can earn our way into heaven. It is grace that inspires us to grow, not growth that purchases grace or favor.—p. 235.

43

It is His [Christ's] grace that gives man power to obey the laws of God. It is this that enables him to break the bondage of evil habits.—ELLEN WHITE,

THE MINISTRY OF HEALING, 115.

Growing in Jesus is indeed the work of a life-time. We all start at different points. We all grow at different rates. And we all need to keep growing. None of us have a character that is perfectly Christlike. . . .

But the fact that we need to keep growing is not to be an occasion for discouragement. . . . We are encouraged to find both the desire to keep grow-ing and the grace that keeps us committed to growth within the family of faith.—p. 236.

44

$\mathcal{T}$he world is perishing for want of the gospel. . . .
The Lord desires that His word of grace shall be
brought home to every soul.—ELLEN WHITE,

CHRIST'S OBJECT LESSONS, 228, 229.

*G*race is the *center* position in our faith, the *core* to which both the extremes of legalism and lawlessness need to return. . . . Grace is at the *heart* of the church doctrine that came out of the Reformation, . . . the center of Adventist theology.

—pp. 236, 237.

45

*W*ithout the grace of Christ every soul would
have been bankrupt for eternity.—Ellen White,

Testimonies to Ministers, 166.

*W*e've been so fearful of losing our identity as keepers of the law, so worried that we might undermine the commitment to obey, so concerned that we might fail to uphold the Sabbath, that we are now used to saying, "Yes, we are saved by grace alone, but . . ." Our members are confused on what we believe about salvation. Sadly, in the pew, the "but" has become more indicative of our doctrine than the "grace."—p. 237.

*T*he sweetest melodies that come from God through human lips—justification by faith, and the righteousness of Christ.—Ellen White,

Review and Herald, April 4, 1893.

*S*omeday we'll all be changed in a moment, in the twinkling of an eye. Until then, we have two desperate needs: to grow more and more like Jesus, and to accomplish that growth in the security and acceptance of His everlasting grace.—p. 237.

*T*he grace of Christ is unlimited, it is God's free gift. . . . There is sunshine in the heart for all who will accept Christ.—Ellen White, *Testimonies for the Church,*

vol. 9, 226.

*W*e're afraid that an emphasis on God's grace will lessen our commitment to obedience, to living the sanctified life, to keeping the commandments, to remembering the Sabbath day to keep it holy. . . . If we Christians are doing poorly in our sanctification (and we certainly are), it is not because we are emphasizing grace too much. It is because we are not emphasizing grace enough!—p. 250.

48

*W*hen the fullness of the time had come, the Deity was glorified by pouring upon the world a flood of healing grace that was never to be obstructed or withdrawn till the plan of salvation should be fulfilled.—ELLEN WHITE, *GOD'S AMAZING GRACE*, 11.

*T*his is the moment when every song we sing should soar with the melodies and harmonies of amazing grace, when every publication should announce "God's grace in all its truth" (Colossians 1:6), when every ministry should proclaim, "Grace and peace be yours in abundance" (1 Peter 1:2). This can be the era of the everlasting "gospel of God's grace" (Acts 20:24) given to "every nation, tribe, language and people" (Revelation 14:6).—p. 251.

49

The purpose and plan of grace existed from all eternity. . . . Redemption was not an afterthought . . . but an eternal purpose to be wrought out for the blessing not only of this atom of a world but for the good of all the worlds which God has created.—Ellen White, *God's Amazing Grace*, 129.

*W*hatever our emphasis has been before, whatever our fundamental focus, now is the time to put everything else in its proper place, to stop being afraid of God's enduring grace, and to fully embrace the everlasting gospel.—p. 252.

*I*n Christ's name our petitions ascend to the Father. He intercedes in our behalf, and the Father lays open all the treasures of His grace for our appropriation, for us to enjoy and impart to others. "Ask in My name," Christ says. ". . . This will give your prayers efficiency, and the Father will give you the riches of His grace."—ELLEN WHITE,

TESTIMONIES FOR THE CHURCH, VOL. 8, 178.

$\mathcal{T}$he treasure of grace will give us the definition of self we so desperately need to know. It is grace that destroys our fear of God and establishes our relationship with Him. It is grace that builds the sure foundation to everything we do—our family life, our work, our church involvement. It is grace that lends wonder and relevance to our beliefs. It is grace that transforms us. It is grace that gives us lasting joy.—p. 252.

51

*E*ven before the prayer is uttered of the yearnings of the heart made known, grace from Christ goes forth to meet the grace that is working upon the human soul.—ELLEN WHITE, *CHRIST'S OBJECT LESSONS*, 206.

The everlasting gospel insists that God chose us in Jesus before the beginning of the world (Ephesians 1:4), before our obedience or good works, before we had even responded to God. The gospel repeats the fact that our inheritance has been prepared for us since the creation of the world (Matthew 25:34), long before we were born. It reveals that God's love is *unfailing,* that it lasts *for ever* (Psalm 52:8).—p. 254.

*D*ivine grace is needed at the beginning, divine grace at every step of advance, and divine grace alone can complete the work.—ELLEN WHITE,

GOD'S AMAZING GRACE, 220.

*T*he everlasting gospel—the good news that Jesus has been thinking about you and me since before the beginning of our world, that He's been planning your home and mine, the place where we'll be living ten million years from now, and that He has made it all possible by what He has done on our behalf—is the sum and substance, the alpha and the omega, the core and center and essence of why Christians are Christians and of why Chris-

tians so love to share their story with people who have not yet heard it.—p. 255.

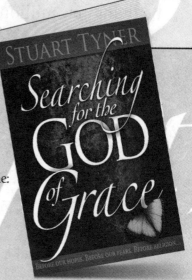